THE FIVE GOLDEN RULES *of* PARENTING

Your Children Are a Gift from God—
How You Raise Them Is Your Gift to Him

MICHELE UNGER

ISBN 978-1-64258-250-5 (paperback)
ISBN 978-1-64258-251-2 (digital)

Christian Faith Publishing, Inc.
832 Park Avenue
Meadville, PA 16335
www.christianfaithpublishing.com

Printed in the United States of America

PREFACE

A simple prayer started it all.

From the pain of my own wounded upbringing, all alone in a hospital room, holding my firstborn infant daughter, came a simple prayer, a desperate cry to God for help. "The legacy that was handed to me, let it stop with me. Don't let me pass it on to the next generation. Show me what to do." God heard my cry and answered me. He not only showed me what to do with my daughter but also with my son, who was born a few years later. God ended the legacy that was handed to me and gave me a new one. Now almost thirty years later, my kids are whole. We are a close family, and most importantly, they know and love God and are walking closely with Him. You see, He really does make all things new, as He is true to His Word (Revelation 21:5).

As I crossed the finish line of raising my own kids, God put on my heart the desire to teach others what He showed me. From that, the Legacy Parenting Class was born in the fall of 2013. The information found in this book and in the class is His information, not my own, taken from the things He taught me while raising my own children. The Golden Rules that are found in these pages are the first lessons I teach in the class; the foundation that everything else taught is built upon. They are the starting point where all parenting needs to begin.

The idea to write this book came about as I was teaching the classes over the last few years. I would often hear from parents, "You should make a video or write a book so I can see or read the information to refresh my memory." Write a complete book with all the information I teach? Make a video? Sounds daunting since I'm not a professional writer. But because they are easily implemented, I thought I'd put the Golden Rules into a book for parents to reference when they need some reminders of these important rules. For those who never attended a Legacy Parenting Class, I believe you'll find these rules are basic and easy to follow and will be amazed at the results you get once you implement them con-sistently. I often hear from attendees of my class that they have them taped to their refrigerator for quick reference.

It is my desire as you read this book that you glean some insight into your own parenting.

Obviously, reading one little book isn't going to fix every issue you encounter in your years as a parent. Parenting is not easy. It is one of the hardest jobs there is, but it is also one of the most rewarding jobs you'll ever love. But if you're struggling with your parenting, unsure of what to do or how or when to discipline, I believe you will find help in these pages. Most of the difficulty I observe in parenting can be traced back to at least one or more of these Golden Rules being broken. It is my hope as you read this book that you will find clarity so you can make the correct changes in how you relate to your child. As you do make these changes, I believe you will experience not only a more peaceful home but a more enjoyable relationship with your child as well.

ACKNOWLEDGMENTS

I am so thankful to God every day for not only making me a mom to Elizabeth and Daniel but for hearing the prayer I prayed in that hospital room and stepping in to help me and change my children's legacy. Thank you doesn't seem enough for all He has done in my life, and I am overwhelmed by his goodness toward me, as well as his love and faithfulness. All I can do to show Him my gratitude is to try to help others with what He has shown me, and in return, bring glory to His name.

My husband, Chris, has not only been one of my biggest encouragers in the writing of this book but also supports me in the parenting classes, sitting by my side as I teach, offering his input and wisdom. We have jokingly called him "my agent" while writing this book, as he did all the tiring leg work, researching publishers, and overseeing all the details that are necessary for taking a manuscript from computer to hard copy. This book would not have been realized if it wasn't for him using his administrative gifts to help me, as I would have found it too daunting. Thank you for being God's perfect gift for me—the love of my life and my helpmate in raising two amazing kids. The best is yet to come.

Elizabeth and Daniel, I am honored to be your mom. Thank you for all your help and encouragement while writing this book and for giving me permission to use examples from your childhood not only in my classes but in this book as well. Elizabeth, your help with writing and editing has been immeasurable and has added so much to the book. Daniel, thank you for offering your expertise and knowledge about the publishing world and also the ins and outs of the bookstore world as well. Your guidance has been instrumental. Both of you have grown into two amazing adults that have taught me so much. Thank you. I love you to the moon and back.

Special thanks go to some wonderful friends who are still in the middle of raising their own children and offered to read my finished manuscript to give me some much-needed feedback. Tom and Andrea Vella, Brittani Blachford, and Josh and Becky Sorensen, your suggestions, help, and support have been priceless and are greatly appreciated. Thank you for taking the time out of your busy lives to help me with this project.

Lastly, to all the amazing parents still in the middle of the race. God is your source and your strength. If you seek Him in your parenting, He will guide you and help you, just as He did to me. God bless you as you raise the next generation for Him and His glory.

CONTENTS

Introduction..13

Chapter 1: Rule # 1: Equal Balance of

          Love and Discipline 21

Chapter 2: Rule #2: Never Reward Bad Behavior...29

Chapter 3: Rule #3: Always Follow Through........46

Chapter 4: Rule #4: How You Say Something

          Is as Important as What You Say 62

Chapter 5: Rule #5: Catch Them Being Good 69

Chapter 6: The Essentials.....................................73

Epilogue: Encouragement for Parents...................83

INTRODUCTION

Many Christian parents today are struggling. Let's face it, parenting is one of the toughest jobs on the planet, and children don't come with a how-to manual. To compound the problem, as parents of multiple children can tell you, you may have ten children and not one of them is exactly the same, each one completely different with different personalities, temperaments, interests, and abilities. What works with one child may or may not work with another.

Then, add to that the difficulty in finding the balance between love and discipline. I've noticed when teaching my parenting class, many parents struggle with discipline. A question I often hear is, "How do I know what boundaries to set or what consequences to give?" Let's be honest, parenting takes courage, and with the way the world is today, more courage is needed than previous generations had to muster.

Many parents also struggle with different fears, one being fear of their child's response to their disciplinary actions. I often hear, "But they'll be mad at me if I do that." They also fear others' criticisms because no one else is parenting that way. Then there's the fear of letting go as their children get older. "What freedoms or privileges are they ready for?" is a question they grapple with as they struggle not to hover.

And what about freedoms and privileges? All parents naturally want to "give good gifts to their children" as the Bible states (Matthew 7:11), but we often go overboard without realizing it, and we become more interested in their comfort than their character development. We sometimes inadvertently make decisions that give the impression that their happiness is more important than their holiness, unintentionally giving them mixed signals. In addition to all these other questions, Christian parents will ask, "How do I help my kids love and know God and live for Him?" This question reveals what, for many, is the real heart's desire, but they grapple with how to make it a reality.

Fortunately, for all of us, in the midst of this confusion, God doesn't leave us alone with our questions. His Word offers all parents the hope, guidance, and direction we're looking for. In the Bible, we can learn much from observing how God, the ultimate parent, parents His own children—namely us.

I begin both the toddler and the adolescent class in my Legacy Parenting Classes with the five Golden Rules that are found in this book. Why do I call them the *Golden* Rules? Because they are the rules that should be consistently present through all the years of parenting, starting before the toddler years all the way through to the age of eighteen. As a matter of fact, they are so important that almost 100 percent of the time, the difficulties parents are experiencing in raising their children can almost always be traced back to at least one or more of these rules being broken.

If as you read through this book you discover that you haven't been using one or more of these rules in your parenting, don't be discouraged. It is never too late to start implementing them. It might be harder at first to correct bad habits in yourself or even more so in your child, who has gotten used to your old way of doing things, but in time, if you are consistent, you should see positive changes in your child's behavior. But you must be consistent—that is key.

The first rule, "There must be an equal balance of love and discipline," is first for a reason. It's first because it is the cornerstone of all the other rules. The remaining rules define this rule; in essence, they demonstrate how to balance love and discipline. Your children must know they are loved, but they also need to know you are the authority in their lives. Starting at their earliest age, both of these aspects must be in equal balance.

If you examine your own parenting style, you will find you or your spouse usually lean more toward one or the other. I often notice in my classes, that many Christian parents especially have a natural inclination toward the love part of parenting. They find that easier than knowing when or how to discipline. They emphasize love more, believing their children will feel more emotionally secure. This is not wrong, and of course, children do feel secure when loved and affirmed. But what many parents don't realize is that children also feel a sense of security when they know you love them enough to discipline them properly and not allow them to be in control. Although they try to get their own way, children have an innate sense that they shouldn't be the ones running the show. They feel insecure when you let them push boundaries they know they shouldn't be able to push. God says in His Word that He "disciplines those He loves" (Hebrews 12:6). This means His discipline of us is actually evidence of His love, that we belong to Him. This is true also of our relationship with our own children. Discipline, done properly, is evidence of our love.

All the Golden Rules work together and need to be used consistently. If you exclude only *one* of the rules from your parenting or break a rule even once or twice when a situation demands it, you will notice problems develop pretty quickly. As you may have discovered, children are pretty smart. From an early age, they go on a recon mission (I will explain this later) to gather information about you. They observe you and your response in various situations. From that, they learn how to manipulate you and their environment to get what they want. They will test you to see your response, and depending on that response, they will learn what they can get away with and what they can't, what you will tolerate and what you won't. With every reaction, you are teaching your child not only who you are but also what is allowed and what is not, which is why consistency is so important starting at an early age (as early as the crawling stage).

There's one thing I'd like to reiterate here before we go any further. As you're reading through this booklet, if you start to realize that you haven't been enforcing some of these Golden Rules, it is never too late to start. Though it is best and makes life much easier for you if these rules are implemented beginning at the earliest stages, if you haven't been applying them in your parenting, look to God for guidance and start implementing them today. It's never too late (Isaiah 43: 18–19).

God gives us guidelines to follow in His Word, and you will notice the Golden Rules are indicative of the way he "raises" us. His interactions with us demonstrate an equal balance of love and discipline. He never rewards our bad behavior. He always follows through on what He says. In other words, when he says something, he does it (Psalm 33:9). His tone with us at times can be firm but also loving. He promises to always reward our obedience, if not now, then in heaven. In other words, He notices our obedience, i.e., catches us being good (Mark 9:41).

Now, before we begin, there's something I feel I need to mention. As you're reading through this book, I never want it to seem as if I had it all figured out or I never seemed to have any weaknesses or problems in my parenting. All parents experience difficulty at one time or another, myself included. But as I previously mentioned at the beginning of this book, I knew I was so emotionally wounded from my own upbringing. This is why I cried out to God in desperation. I also knew from first-hand experience the power a parent yields in a child's life, the damage that can be done to a child's heart and mind. It's exactly because I was weak and I knew it that I depended so completely on God and His wisdom and guidance and clung to Him while raising our children. Because I had no idea what I was doing, I was willing to do whatever He told me to do, which is one of the reasons why, I believe, He did speak so clearly to me; He knew I would obey whatever He told me to do, no questions asked. This book is not about me. It's all about God and what He can do in anyone's life who puts their trust in Him and leans on Him for all their needs, whether that be parenting or anything else. His power and resources are endless, and He can break any and every chain. He broke the legacy that was handed to me and gave our family a new one. Every parent reading this book can have hope and know that what He did for me He will do for you if you ask Him and then obey what He tells you to do. He alone gets all the glory and praise not only for how my kids turned out but for what you're about to read in the following pages.

Having said that, the following rules are the rules He gave me while raising my own children, and I know they work if you apply them consistently. I have heard from many parents who, after taking the class and then applied the golden rules at home, were amazed at the results. Let's discuss them and see why they are so important in parenting our children.

CHAPTER 1

Rule # 1: Equal Balance of Love and Discipline

There are two things your child needs to grasp in their earliest understanding of you, and those two things must be in equal balance.

First, they need to know that you love them totally and unconditionally, that you are a safe person, and that they can trust you to care for them emotionally, physically, and spiritually.

Second, they need to know you are the authority in their life and if they disobey you, there will be consequences.

Why is it so important that these be in equal balance? Because if there is too much love and not enough discipline when needed, your child will learn to be spoiled and selfish. Children are born with a sin nature. We are all born believing it is all about us.

By nature, we are born with a selfish, self-centered attitude. Proverbs 22:15 teaches us, "Foolishness is bound up in the heart of a child, but the rod of correction will drive it far from him." It has been said that God's love is not a pampering love but a perfecting love. Since children are born selfish, it is our job to teach them to be otherwise, but too much love and not enough discipline will reinforce their selfish tendencies.

What does too much love look like? Well, rewarding bad behavior is one way. Let's say you tell your child they need to finish their homework before they can watch TV, but they don't complete their homework because they were goofing off. Then they start crying because they're going to miss their favorite program. If you let them watch TV anyway because they're crying and you feel bad that they're going to miss their show, this is in essence "an enabling love." You are rewarding bad behavior. I once observed a neighbor correct her child, and the child responded by sticking her tongue out at her mom. The mom's response was to roll her eyes and then proceed to do nothing. This lack of discipline of her child at that moment is not only *not* loving her child; it is encouraging bad behavior in the future. The mom's response taught her daughter the behavior was acceptable and pretty much guaranteed worse behavior in the future, as her daughter will test other boundaries.

Besides not disciplining when the situation calls for it, too much love shows itself in many other ways. Other examples would be purchasing everything your child wants or not setting boundaries by letting them interrupt your conversations with others, whether you're on the phone or speaking face-to-face, dropping everything the moment your children want something from you. When we do these things, we are inadvertently telling them they are the center of the universe. Children need to know they are important and a priority but the world does not revolve around them. Your child needs to hear you say the word *no* or *wait* at times. They also need to learn others, including you, have needs as well, not just them.

When we don't set boundaries, we are not balancing love with discipline. We are being too heavy with *love*, if that is even the correct word. I say that because if your child needs discipline, correction, or boundaries and you respond in a passive way, may I boldly suggest that you're not really being loving? As I mentioned before, the Bible states in Hebrews 12:6 that "God disciplines those he loves." Discipline is evidence of his love. But it also further states that if

God doesn't discipline us, then we don't really belong to him. We are illegitimate children (Hebrews 12:8). His discipline of us is proof we belong to him, that we are His. You are your child's primary teacher, and from you, they need to learn so many things in the few years they are with you. One of them is to respect authority and what appropriate and acceptable behavior looks like.

However, after saying that, if there is too much discipline and not enough love, you will be left with a frustrated child. Ephesians 6:4 says, "And you fathers, do not provoke your children to wrath, but bring them up in the training and admonition of the Lord." There are many ways we can frustrate our children, provoking them to wrath, but one way is when we are always disciplining them and being on them for every little infraction. We can overdo it with our parenting and end up frustrating them. Being overly heavy in our discipline is one way.

I have witnessed this. I remember a time we were entertaining guests in our home and they brought with them their two young sons, both early elementary school age. The boys could barely breathe without their father, correcting them for every infraction. If they walked too fast while going from room to room, didn't say "Thank you" for every small gesture, or got too excited while playing with our son, Daniel, the father would repeatedly correct them in front of everyone. Constantly. I could see the frustration in the young boys' eyes as they consistently tried to obey their father's orders but they could never seem to please him.

Sometimes children are just being children. We have all heard the saying "Pick your battles." In parenting, this is very true, and parents need wisdom in deciding when the battle is something worth picking. Children should be reprimanded sparingly and only when the situation demands it, as in when they are being outright disobedient, rebellious, or testing boundaries. To overdo it frustrates children and is an example of too much discipline. Sometimes we need to give our children some wiggle room to be kids and overlook certain actions, especially if they are not being outright disobedient.

As far as the love part goes, your home should be a place of laughter and fun. There should be lots of hugs and kisses, words of affirmation and praise. Your children should hear you tell them often that you love them and that you're glad God gave them to you. Quality time spent with them also demonstrates love and is very important in making a child feel secure. This doesn't have to include spending money and often shouldn't. Playing board games, doing puzzles, baking cookies or enjoying a favorite hobby, watching movies together as a family (with popcorn, of course), riding bikes, going on picnics, taking a walk in the park, or throwing a baseball or Frisbee around (the list is endless) are all ways you can show your child that you love them and enjoy spending time with them.

In the Bible, Solomon reminds us in Proverbs 1:7, "The fear of the Lord is the beginning of wisdom." We understand what this means, and it doesn't make us cower in fear. It doesn't mean that we are afraid of God that He will harm us. It means we have a healthy respect and understanding of who He is versus who we are. He is God, and we are not. We reverence Him and obey Him, and we know that if we don't, we will experience negative consequences because he loves us. In many respects, this should be true of your relationship with your child. There should be a healthy respect and understanding of who you are in their lives, and they should be taught to obey you. My children had a healthy "fear" of my husband and me as their parents. They knew we required obedience from them, or they would experience consequences. They also knew us to be loving and fun and safe. These two qualities need to be in balance.

I'm witnessing though, a disturbing trend lately, where it seems parents have a fear of their kids and not the other way around. Parents bribing kids to keep them quiet or to get them to do what they request or being afraid of their child having a meltdown or tantrum and bending over backwards to prevent one from happening. I witnessed this on a popular television program recently. The parent on the screen was offering their child ice cream in order to encourage them to get ready for bed without a tantrum. While working recently, I witnessed a child who was not ready to leave the store where I work when the mom told him it was time to leave. He proceeded to say no and then calmly lay down on the floor right in front of the cash register. He lay there prostrate in a very cramped store while other shoppers had to walk around him. The mom stood there making excuses for his behavior and said sheepishly, "He's not ready to leave yet," while she chatted with him, asking him occasionally, "Are you ready to go now?" She then proceeded to calmly wait until the three-year-old prince had decided he was ready to leave, which took about five minutes. This is obviously an example of a child not fearing the parent. I think we all will agree a three-year-old should not be calling the shots.

Now, it's at this point in the class that I'm usually asked "So, how do you get them to fear and respect you in a healthy way and thereby, obey you?" The next three Golden Rules will demonstrate how this is achieved.

CHAPTER 2

Rule #2: Never Reward Bad Behavior

May I emphasize this again? Never, under any circumstances, should you reward bad behavior! Now, you might be thinking, "Well, duh, Michele." But you would be surprised how many parents don't even realize that they are breaking this rule. They break it with toddlers, and they break it with their teenagers. It's probably the rule that is broken most often, along with not following through. Of course, it looks different in each case, which is why it is often not recognized.

What does "rewarding bad behavior" look like, and why is it so important not to reward it?

For a toddler, it would go something like this: You are in a grocery store with your toddler. At the checkout line, your child asks you for a candy bar, and you tell them, "No, not this time," and then they throw themselves on the floor and have an all-out tantrum right there on the floor. They, of course, do this because they know they have a better chance of getting what they want in front of a crowd of witnesses. After all, you'll do anything at this point to shut them up. Yes, they are that smart! Rewarding bad behavior would be handing them the candy bar to shut them up. You should never, under any circumstances, give them the candy bar or anything else they want. As a matter of fact, they should be taken outside if necessary for you to deal with them. They need to experience negative consequences when they misbehave.

Another example would be the example I ended the previous chapter with (the little boy who was allowed to stay on the floor until he felt ready to leave). The mom not disciplining him by picking him up and taking him outside to correct him was actually rewarding bad behavior, or in other words, rewarding him with what *he* was demanding (i.e., staying the store until he was ready to leave). You are the authority, and your child needs to obey you; when you say it's time to leave, they leave.

Why is it so dangerous to reward bad behavior? Because if you do, you have just made your life that much harder. Having success once, they will remember your response in the future, knowing that if they push hard enough in the next situation, they will get what they want. They will repeat the behavior. If your child refuses to eat his dinner and then requests a cookie, and you reward him with that cookie (because you reason he'll starve to death if he doesn't eat something and after all at least he's eating a cookie), you will have just ensured a repeat offense; he will refuse to eat his dinner the next time until you give into his demands. You might laugh, but my husband and I have witnessed this. One of my husband's relatives, while trying to feed their two-year-old who refused to eat, gave him a cupcake because she insisted "it's all he'll eat plus; it's better than nothing." They were correct; it was all he would eat. Why? Because they had taught him at a young age that he could manipulate mom and dad. He knew if he refused to eat long enough and then threw in a tantrum if they persisted in trying to feed him anything other than what he wanted, they would eventually give into his demands. So this ritual continued at every meal.

So even if you hold out in the beginning and initially say no to your child's request for a cookie but give in after a while to calm him down when he starts screaming uncontrollably, the lesson you have taught him then is "If Mom or Dad initially says no, if I carry on long enough, Mom and Dad have a breaking point and will eventually give in." Now having success, this behavior will be repeated the next time. If you have told them no and they act up, there needs to be a firm response and consequences if it continues (below I discuss how to know which consequences to choose). You must be tougher than them. Under no circumstances should you ever give into their demands.

You need to keep reminding yourself during the first few years of your child's life that your child is gathering information about you. These are the years you are demonstrating who you are to them. You are either intentionally or unintentionally setting up patterns of behavior, yours and theirs, in the early years that will indicate what the remaining years in your home will look like. Children are preservationists: they are all about preserving their own comfort. If it costs them to misbehave, they will remember that and will think twice about repeating in the future the behavior that brought them discomfort. They will say to themselves, "Self, that didn't work out too well for you. Might want to rethink that response next time." They are less likely to repeat it in the future. This is why consistency is so important. If they do repeat it in the future, then your response needs to be consistent each and every time until they get the message their behavior will not be tolerated.

Have you ever watched *Supernanny* on television? When Jo Frost is teaching the parents how to discipline, she will use the naughty spot to put the child when they are disobeying. If you notice, sometimes she will have the parent put the child back in the naughty spot twenty-plus times (restarting the time-out clock over again) until the child stays put for their timeout. It looks exhausting, and it can be, but eventually the child gets the message and stays put for the duration. She will do the same when teaching the parents how to keep their children in bed at night. Consistency in parenting can be tiring but always eventually pays off. You have to be tougher than them, more stubborn and strong-willed than they are. I would tell my son, almost humorously, when he repeatedly acted up, "You think you're stubborn? I invented the word!"

On a side note, when teaching the class, one of the things I teach in the "essentials" section of the class (and discussed further in this book) is how to know what discipline to use. Unlike Jo Frost, I personally don't believe in using the naughty spot or any one specific discipline for every child in every situation, a "one size fits all" mentality so to speak. I teach that in order for discipline to be effective, you must understand what matters most to your child and be willing to use it in your discipline. It must cost them to disobey. Every child is different, and each situation is different. If you always put your child in their room for every infraction, a question I ask is, "What if they like being in their room?"

Our son, Daniel, didn't necessarily *like* being in his bedroom, but he was the kind of kid that when life gave you lemons you made lemonade. He just found something to occupy himself while he was in there. It wasn't something that bothered him all that much. As my daughter, Elizabeth, got a little older, she actually loved being in her room. So you need to study your child to figure out what they care about most and then have the courage to use it. If you choose something that isn't important to them, you won't get their attention and rarely will the behavior change. The thing they value most might be a favorite toy, a favorite television program, a favorite sport or activity, a favorite ritual they enjoy with you, like you reading them a book every night before bed. Maybe putting them in their room, not allowing them to go outside to play or even not allowing them to go to a party. The choices are endless, and it's up to you to know what that is for each child. The thing you use will also change over time as they change and grow. With my son, Daniel, it seemed I was changing the thing I used every few months. As his interests in different toys or activities changed, so did my choices.

So what does not rewarding bad behavior for an older child look like? How might this play out as a teenager? In a myriad of ways. Let's say your teenager is irresponsible and has demonstrated they can't be trusted. To reward bad behavior would be to give them privileges they haven't shown they can handle nor deserve. An example might be dropping your pre-teen off at the mall unsupervised for the afternoon or handing your sixteen-year-old the keys to the family car with no restrictions. They haven't earned that kind of trust. What if they are prone to laziness and won't hold down a job? Rewarding bad behavior would be to give them the money to go to the movies with friends or to buy them those expensive sneakers they want instead of requiring them to get a job.

Sometimes rewarding bad behavior in a teenager can be more subtle. I have talked with moms whose children seem to make a habit of forgetting items they need to bring to school. Sports equipment, lunch, schoolwork, you name it. If this behavior is rare or happens only once in a while, then, of course, it's okay to help them out by bringing the item to school for them but only once in a while. But if you notice this is becoming a habit, then to continue to rescue your child by bringing the item to school is not only rewarding bad behavior, but it is enabling them to continue to forget and not learn to be responsible.

I have spoken with parents whose children actually got angry with them because they didn't drop everything and rush the forgotten item to school. If that is the case, to reward the behavior by dropping the item off is not only enabling bad behavior but also encourages an entitlement attitude in your child as well. Often the most loving thing you can do in these situations is to let them experience the negative consequences such as being unable to participate in practice after school or receiving a bad mark on a homework assignment. As a parent, this can be one of the hardest things to do, letting your child experience pain, but it is also the most loving. Think about it—when your child is an adult, life will not be as kind or understanding to them. One of our jobs is to prepare them for life. If they are irresponsible on the job, they will be fired. If they forget something in college, the professor will give them a failing grade. We need to prepare them for life now.

I need to state something here about the behavior traits like irresponsibility or lack of trust mentioned above and other ones like them. If you continue over time to reward bad behavior with your child into the teenage years, a habit will form and can be imprinted on their character. In the same way, if you notice these or other negative qualities in your child and do nothing to try to alter those qualities, *over time through discipline and correction*, they will most likely carry those qualities into adulthood. So generally, if you see your child is heading in the wrong direction (e.g., irresponsible, untrustworthy, or lazy) and you don't alter that direction with discipline, they usually will continue to be irresponsible, untrustworthy, and lazy. Sadly, I have seen this over and over again. It must cost them to be irresponsible. It must cost them to be lazy or untrustworthy.

Most children will not just naturally change as they get older or become more mature as they age as many parents mistakenly believe. This is why if *you* don't alter the negative direction they are heading, then they will continue down that path. It's human nature. We often don't change what we're doing unless it brings pain or discomfort to our lives. This is why God will often allow difficulty or suffering (i.e., discipline) to get our attention and correct our course, because He loves us and knows the direction we're headed will bring destruction. We need to do the same with our children because we love them and want the best for them. We need to put pressure on them and make them uncomfortable with where they are. A child who is irresponsible at ten or twelve will become an irresponsible eighteen-year-old if uncorrected. I have unfortunately seen this time and time again. Unfortunately, it is much more difficult to change course and correct a behavior in an eighteen-year-old than it is when they're twelve. You will have less leverage in their lives.

Can a person change once they're an adult? Of course they can, and many of us can attest to that fact. Our God is all about change and turning around lives, making beauty out of ashes (Isaiah 61:3). A small percentage also might make positive changes in their behavior when the natural consequences of life hits them and they, let's say, lose a job for being irresponsible. Often though, the world isn't as tolerant with our children as we are, and if we don't discipline them to correct their course, the world will when they become adults.

Isn't it easier to be trained from an early age to be responsible and trustworthy as their characters are being formed than to experience the pain and difficulty of failing and then trying to change an entrenched bad habit as an adult? This is after all our main responsibility as parents, to teach. The Bible states in Proverbs 22:6, "Train up a child in the way they should go, and when they are old they will not depart from it." Let me provide an example from our own experience as parents.

Hershey Park

My son, Daniel, was not completely trustworthy as he was growing up. We sometimes caught him in lies, and he often didn't follow through when asked to do a task around the house. We would get the "I forgot" excuse. Although we emphasized how important trust was in our relationship with him, and of course, we disciplined him when he was irresponsible, it still wasn't quite sinking in. I knew as he approached adolescence that it would be important for us to trust him since he would be spending more time away from us and be more independent of us. So I watched for something I could use to finally get his attention in this area. This is what I mean when I say you need to make it cost them. If you choose a consequence they don't really care about, it usually will not bring about much change. We had been disciplining Daniel for a while on these issues, but it wasn't bringing lasting change. You have to have the courage to use the things that matter most to them in order to get their attention and give them the motivation they need to make changes in their life. I knew as he got older there would be things he was going to want to do or privileges he was going to want, things that mattered to him. So I kept an eye out for something to use that he valued in order to teach him.

God provided such an opportunity for us. We had just dropped our seventeen-year-old daughter off at church to go on a mission trip to Russia, and I was alone in the car with Daniel. Seeing his sister get the privilege of going off without us to another country must have inspired him, so he blurted out, "I can't wait till next year when we get to go to Hershey Park without our parents!" Our children's school held an eighth-grade class trip to the amusement park where they could roam with their friends without adult supervision. I knew I had him! The trip was still a year away. If Daniel was mentioning a trip that was still a year away, then it must be really important to him.

I reminded Daniel of all the times we had disciplined him in the past and how we had repeatedly reminded him of how important it was for us to trust him as he got older if he was going to want privileges. I reminded him that we had told him then, without that trust he wouldn't have privileges in the future. I said that all that had brought us to this moment. Because he was not completely trustworthy, I told him he would not be allowed to go to Hershey Park the following year unless we saw some changes in him. I could tell I had his attention. "After all," I said, "how do we know you won't check your brain at the door and stand up on a roller coaster because your friends challenge you to? How do we know you'll show up at the check-in with teachers during the day when they tell you to?" I laid out a list of specific things I needed to see change in his life before we would let him go. It is important to be specific and not general when stating what you require of them, so they clearly understand what the goals are. I also told him we would not be making our decision until right before we had to sign the permission slip, so he had almost a year to make these changes and show us we could trust him.

I was willing to use it to teach him these valuable life lessons because we love him and want the

41

best for his life. This takes a lot of courage on the part of parents because we want to naturally "give good gifts to our children" (Matthew 7:11), as the Bible states. We love to see them happy. So to withhold something they love or are looking forward to or to be willing to mess with the things they care about most can be really difficult. Who said parenting was easy? But isn't that what God does with us? He loves us too much to leave us the way we are. He cares more about our holiness than our happiness, and He is willing to sacrifice the latter to bring about the former. His motivation for this is not to punish us or to bring us pain. His motivation is love. He is willing to do what is best for us even if it brings us temporary pain. We must be willing to do the same. We have to care more about their character than their comfort and the future benefits over the present convenience.

Would it have broken my heart to withhold Hershey Park from him? Yes! But the lessons learned and his character development was more important to us. If a year later he was not able to go to Hershey Park because he decided not to make the changes that we had specifically laid out for him, then it was by his own choice. I had laid out specific things he had to do, all of them attainable and all of them age appropriate. If he didn't go, we wouldn't be withholding the trip from him; he would by his own decision. He would only have himself to blame. I was willing for him to miss the trip if that is what it took to finally teach him this important character trait we had been trying to instill in him. Yes, I would've been sad he missed the trip. But even more than missing the trip, I would've been even more sad that He missed an opportunity for personal growth in his own life if he decided not to make the changes to become trustworthy. It really was a heart issue.

On a side note, because I always followed through (see rule #3) and never made idle threats, he knew I meant business. This would not have worked if we had not always shown our kids we meant what we said and followed through in the past. Remember, I said in the beginning that all the rules have to be consistently followed. Because we didn't reward bad behavior and always followed through with consequences for the previous twelve years, Daniel knew not to test me. He knew I was willing, if necessary, to withhold the trip from him.

How did it work out? Well, it goes to show that with the right motivation you can accomplish anything. With the trip, I had finally found the right motivation. The child who for years couldn't seem to remember anything miraculously and instantaneously remembered everything. He did what he was supposed to do when he was supposed to do it. The lying stopped. How can I be sure the possibility of losing the trip was his motivation? Because not even two weeks into it, he asked me if I noticed the changes in his behavior. He would check back with me periodically over the next year to make sure I was still aware of the changes he was making in his life. About a month before we needed to make the decision, he approached me and said, "Mom, I know you're not going to make the decision for another month, but if you had to decide today, would I be able to go?" I told him I was so proud of him and the changes he had made and if I had to decide that day, yes, he would be able to go, but he still had a month until I decided. He was beaming!

Not only did Daniel become responsible enough to go on the class trip, but basically, he became over-the-top responsible! And not only for that year until the Hershey Park trip but for the rest of his life up until the present day, now at the ripe old age of twenty-five. They say if you do anything for eight weeks it becomes a habit. Well, you can imagine what happened if he had to be responsible and trustworthy for a whole year! As a matter of fact, he got a job at the age of fourteen at a local fast food restaurant, became a team leader by the age of sixteen, and by the time he was seventeen, his boss would put Daniel in charge of the store when he was away on vacation. Even I was amazed at how fast and complete the change was in him.

This also shows why you need to use the things they value most to motivate them. He truly valued the trip. If he hadn't, I doubt any real lasting change would've taken place. I truly believe if we hadn't corrected his course with discipline by potentially costing him the trip he desired so much, he would've stayed on the track he was headed. Other things we had done to correct his behavior didn't seem to quite get his attention. If he had stayed on the track he was headed, I also believe it would have not only hindered the job opportunities that were presented to him in the past and the present, but it also would've affected his witness as a Christian. Faithfulness is an important trait for the Christian to possess (1 Corinthians 4:2), as the world watches to see if we are walking what we say we believe. If we had allowed Daniel to go to Hershey Park, knowing he was irresponsible and couldn't be trusted, we would have been rewarding bad behavior, thus ensuring the behavior continued. We also would've missed a golden opportunity that God had given us to correct the direction he was heading and put him on a new path.

CHAPTER 3

Rule #3: Always Follow Through

Let me reemphasize the word *always*! Another way you might say this rule is to "never make idle threats." Basically, when you say something, you need to mean it and do it. It is actually better to never say something (i.e., issue a command, make a request of them, or tell them a consequence you intend to do) than to say something and not follow through on it. You will damage your authority in their lives and your credibility with them, damage that will make your life ten times harder in the future.

As I previously stated, at the earliest age, young children go on a recon mission gathering information about you. Let's think about this. When your cute little bundle arrives, they don't know you from Adam. They squint and stare trying to figure out who this person is that is holding them and gushing all over them. After a few months, as they grow and begin to crawl, they start discovering and exploring their new world. They don't know what is allowed and what isn't. They also don't know you. After all, up until this point, they didn't need any boundaries because they couldn't go anywhere on their own and all they knew of you is that you lovingly met their every need. Whether it was a diaper change when wet or a feeding when hungry, you met that need.

Children want what they want when they want it because they are born with a sin nature that is self-centered. Once they start crawling, they test boundaries. You might tell them no when they reach to touch something they shouldn't touch, but let's face it, they want to touch it, and your words don't mean much to them. What they want to know is "What will happen to me if I touch this thing? Will it be a positive experience or a negative one for me?" After all, in their world, it is all about them. So you say no, and they touch it anyway. How you respond in that moment will determine if your life becomes easier or harder as a parent.

We all are guilty of not following through at one time or another, sometimes just because of exhaustion. Of all the Golden Rules, it seems this is the one that is usually broken the most. This is also the rule that, if broken, seems to not bring out the best in parents, the attractive quality we call yelling. This happens in many different scenarios but is often the result of no follow-through by the parents. Let me give you an example.

When my husband and I were newly married, we lived in a small home. Our backyard backed up to our neighbor's backyard, so we could sit on our back porch and observe the happenings in our neighbor's yard. Both of us worked full time, so in the evening, we loved to just sit on our porch to relax and chat…and watch the entertainment going on in our neighbor's yard. Our neighbor had a two-year-old son (I'll call him Johnny), who loved to play in his sandbox. One day, while we were relaxing on our porch, we noticed Johnny doing just that, playing in his sandbox. His mother stuck her head out the door to call him in for dinner. He didn't budge, continuing to play happily with the sand. A few minutes passed, and she stuck her head out the door again, her voice slightly louder. And again, he didn't budge. Somehow this little boy had already learned at two years old that mom doesn't mean what she says the first couple times she asks him to do something. Without realizing it, she had already trained him and taught him about herself and what she requires of him. What had she taught him unintentionally? That when mom asks you to do something, she's not serious, and you may delay your response until she's asked you three or four times. How do I know this? Because it wasn't until the third time she stuck her head out the door, her voice angrier but not quite at yelling pitch, that he started to stand up, one foot in the sandbox and one foot out. He still didn't move toward the house though, discerning she wasn't quite serious yet. By the fourth time, mom was practically a raving lunatic as she screamed her command to come in one last time, or else! Or else what? I'm not quite sure because she was incoherent at that point. Finally, calm and relaxed, Johnny turned and strolled toward the house, happy as a lark, while mom, I'm sure, bald from pulling her hair out, needed to get an aspirin for her migraine. Maybe this scenario has played itself out at your house. The details might be different, but the end results are the same—a relaxing evening ruined.

What happened? No follow-through. When you issue a command, your child needs to know that you mean it the first time. If you find yourself reaching the yelling point often, then you have lost control, and it's usually because you have broken rule #3.

You might need to reevaluate what you're doing. Your children have learned they don't need to listen to you, and to be honest, you're the one that taught them that. Remember, most kids only care how something affects them, so if there are no negative consequences when they disobey you, they will keep on doing what they're doing. They just tune out the screaming. After all, your screaming doesn't really interfere with their world, just yours. There needs to be consequences when they disobey you, even if it's just a simple request you've made of them. We could tell by observing Johnny that he knew mom didn't really mean it until the third or fourth time she called him. He had no fear of consequences and knew he could ignore her and keep doing what he was doing. How could this incident have been handled differently?

First, when dealing with toddlers, it is best to warn them ahead of time what is going to happen; that way, they are not caught off guard. Children have no concept of time, so they don't do well when something they're enjoying is interrupted unexpectedly. Give your child a warning in advance—something like, "We're going to be eating dinner in ten minutes, so Mommy will be calling you in soon." Then when you call them in, they're expecting it and not surprised.

Next, in a firm voice (not angry), you should issue a command once to come into the house for dinner. Then if your child doesn't come in within a reasonable amount of time, you should issue a second warning, including a consequence if they don't obey you. You could say something like, "Bobby, I asked you to come in for dinner now, and if you don't come in right now, you will be going to your room after dinner." Then if your child doesn't come in, walk outside (without lecturing or yelling and with very few words), tell them the consequence you had stated previously will now be enforced, that he is going to his room after dinner. Take him by the hand or, if needed, carry him inside to dinner. During dinner, so he doesn't forget, you can remind him what the consequence is going to be when he is done eating, and then make sure you follow through.

You may also decide instead to put him in his room for disobeying you *before* eating his dinner. Once he has served his time, he may come out to eat. That choice is up to you. The important thing is to follow through with the consequence you stated.

If he has a tantrum while you are bringing him inside, then put him in his room (or time out) first until he is calm, then once calm, he can come to the table for dinner. You shouldn't allow him to get any more attention by disrupting everyone else's meal with a tantrum. Then after he is done eating, put him in his room for the first offense of not obeying you, reminding him why he is being put there.

Note: The consequence you choose is up to you, but what I recommend is that parents are prepared with what the consequences will be ahead of time. This way, you're not fumbling with what to do if they don't obey and you avoid going overboard with extreme consequences like "You're grounded for life" in a moment of anger. Also, as stated previously, it needs to cost them. You need to know your child and what consequence will affect them. It might be going to their room after dinner (unless they like going to their room), or it might mean they go to bed an hour earlier. You decide what it should be. But the important thing is to pick a consequence that will mean something to them and to follow through on it if they don't obey.

You also need to remember that the early years are the most important years to impress upon them the need to obey you. If you demonstrate at a young age that you mean what you say and that there will be consequences if they disobey you (and consequences they don't like), over time you often will find you won't have to keep proving yourself to them by following through. They usually eventually stop testing you. You have set the groundwork in the early years, and it makes your life so much easier as they get older. When you say something, they will have learned to do it because they know you mean business, especially if you have chosen consequences that mean something to them. Daniel had learned long before that day, I meant it when I told him he wouldn't be going to Hershey Park if he didn't change his ways. He had a history with us and didn't test it. He knew I meant what I said. That is why it was effective. We had always followed through. I didn't have to prove myself to him anymore.

I remember God teaching me the follow-through lesson pretty early in my parenting. Now, you would've thought, after watching what transpired with Johnny, I would've learned the lesson of follow-through long before I had my own kids. But like I said, we often don't realize we are unintentionally breaking these rules, so God had to teach me as well.

My firstborn, my daughter, Elizabeth, was about the same age Johnny was, which is about two and a half years old. After dinner, all the moms on our street were hanging out on one of the driveways, chatting, as our children all played together. My daughter proceeded to get inside one of those cars children can sit in and decided that no other child could join her. The funny thing is it wasn't even her car! What was I saying about a sinful nature? As other children tried to open the door to come inside, she would grip the doors tightly with her little hands so they couldn't be opened. I warned Elizabeth that if she didn't share, she was going in the house. I continued to chat with the other moms and glanced down to see her continue to push the other children away as she held tightly to the doors. I warned her a second time that she would go in the house if she didn't share and again went back to talking. You should state the command twice, to give them a warning and give them a chance to correct their behavior. As I'm sure you can guess, she still wouldn't budge, so without another word, I went to the car, opened the door, and pulled her out. I placed her in one arm, her bike in another, and off we went toward our house. Immediately she cried, "Okay, okay, Mommy! I'll share!" I was pretty new at this parenting stuff, and my first instinct was to put her down. I reasoned (or should I say, made excuses) to myself that she had learned her lesson, and after all, it was a beautiful evening, and I was enjoying myself getting to know my new neighbors. I wasn't interested in going in the house yet myself.

Sound familiar? Just as I was getting ready to put her down, I heard God whisper clearly to me, "You didn't say you would pick her up for a few seconds and then put her down. You said she was going in the house." I knew He was teaching me something important—that I needed to follow through on what I had said. I responded, "You're right, Lord," and in the house we went.

As I put her in the bathtub to give her a bath, Elizabeth told me with tears in her eyes she was sorry for not listening to me. I told her that I was glad she was sorry but in the future I expected her to listen to me, that when I said something, I meant it. I also told her that if she had listened to me she could've been outside playing with her friends, but now she would have to be in for the rest of the night. She spent the rest of the evening staring out her second-story bedroom window at all her friends playing without her. It taught her an important lesson and made an impression on her. Funny thing, recently Elizabeth read this story in my book and laughed and said she still remembers it. I am convinced, if I had not listened to the still small voice of God and instead put her down when she started crying, it would not have had the same lasting impression on her that it did. I was starting to learn she was a strong-willed child, and she was testing me. Had I failed that test, I know for a fact our lives would have gotten much more difficult. There were many more new tests during her toddler years, and in each one, I had to be consistent, or she would've been running the household! As I said, she was strong-willed. She learned that we were the authority and there would be consequences, and we would follow through with them if she disobeyed us. It made our life a lot easier in the future. God taught me the first of many valuable lessons in parenting that day.

I just gave you two examples of what following through looks like with a toddler, but how about teenagers? With teenagers, the situation might appear more subtle, but it is no less important to follow through with them just as it is with toddlers. Remember though, if you have been following though with consequences since they were toddlers, you won't usually have to be as diligent as they get older because they will have a history with you and already know you mean what you say. Often, a simple reminder when they forget is all it takes to get them back on track.

I remember a few years ago I was teaching a parenting class in a Christian maternity home for teenage mothers. As I was going over the Golden Rules with the girls, one of them spoke up and said she remembered a situation where her parents broke two of the rules with her—to never reward bad behavior and to always follow through. I asked her to explain what she meant.

By her own admission, she said she was an irresponsible teenager. So she was surprised when her parents bought her a cell phone anyway. She realized as we discussed the rules that they were breaking rule #2 (never reward bad behavior). But they also told her that she would have to pay for half the phone bill beginning in three months. She informed me they never made her pay for her part of the phone bill, breaking rule #3 (always follow through). What I found interesting is that this young girl noticed the discrepancy in what her parents said they would do and what they actually did. And just like she noticed this, our children notice when we don't follow through, and they make a mental note of it. They will store it away for the future reference, so when we issue a command or make a request in the future, they have learned it is optional whether they obey us or not.

As parents of teenagers, we often have a habit of issuing "threats" to our kids without thinking about what we're saying. It's just easier because we think if we just tell them the consequences that will happen if they disobey us, that will be enough to encourage obedience. Sometimes it is enough, but often it's not. But if we do that often enough without following through, our teenagers will just tune us out, understanding that there will be no consequences if they ignore us. Then when they ignore us, we end up getting more irritated with them and eventually start yelling. Do you find this occurring in your home? You might say something like, "If you don't do your homework, clean your room, empty the trash cans, etc., you can't go to your friend's house, your basketball game, your party, etc. . ." You fill in the blank. Then they don't do what you requested, but you allow them the rewards anyway. Hence, ignoring your requests in the future continues. This is what's called a "crazy cycle," and eventually, it will end up bringing stress, irritation, and usually a lot of yelling into your home. Without realizing it, the parents are often the cause. It is better to not list a consequence in the first place than to state one and not follow through on it if they ignore you.

Is it okay to repeat the request and give them a warning before you follow through on the consequence? Yes. You could say, "Jimmy, I asked you to clean your room. This is your only warning. If you don't clean your room, you won't be able to go to the party." But if after the second warning they don't comply, you need to enforce the consequence you stated. Is it painful to take away a privilege? Yes, it is. But if you choose the right consequence (i.e., you choose something that costs them, that they value) and you are being consistent with following through, you won't have to do it very often. Remember, kids are preservationists, and they will get the message pretty fast that Mom and Dad mean business. What you end up with is a more peaceful home.

Something that has come up in some of my parenting classes when discussing follow-through is the topic of withholding a sporting event as a consequence. I have had concerned parents admit to me that although the sport their child is playing should be the thing to withhold as a consequence because their child values it the most, they don't want to use it because not only would their child be upset with them, but they would be letting their child's teammates and coach down. I do understand the parents' dilemma that they are possibly letting their team and coach down, but if that sport is really the thing their child values most, then they need to use it. One thing to consider though is if it is truly the *most valued* thing in their child's life, then it won't have to be used more than once because that will get the message across to them loud and clear. Also, you will not be the one withholding the sport; your child will. All they have to do is obey, and they can go to their game. If they choose not to obey, that is their choice. It will also demonstrate that you mean business and have the courage to mess with the things they care about. I do want to state though that if you use this as a consequence, to be fair, I would warn your child in advance that this will be the consequence for future disobedience to give them a chance to change their behavior. Let them know you are willing to use it if you have to.

As far as letting down the coach and teammates that might be depending on your child's participation, that very well might be the case for a game. Like I said, parenting takes courage. But one game doesn't make the season, and if your child does miss the game, not only will it probably only happen once, it is again by their choice. You haven't made them miss a game; they have. You have warned them previously that this would be a consequence of disobedience in the future, so they are in control of whether it happens or not.

A question I often get from parents who haven't been consistently following through but now want to start is, "How do I take control back since my kids are used to not listening to me because I haven't followed through in the past?" What I tell them is to sit your child down and have a discussion with them. Let them know that a new day has dawned. That in the past when you have told them something, you haven't been following through on consequences and you are to blame for that, but that is going to change starting now. Tell them when you make a request of them, you expect them to obey you, but if they don't, there will be consequences, and those consequences will not be pleasant. It's probably best to decide ahead of time what the consequences will be and let them know so they are forewarned ahead of time—especially if, like I said, you are going to use the removal of a sports activity or a party they are looking forward to. Confirm that they understand what you have said. Then in the future, you must make sure that you follow through with what you stated would happen. Consistency is extremely important.

CHAPTER 4

Rule #4: How You Say Something Is as Important as What You Say

Communication, it has been said, is made up of not just the words we speak but also the tone of our voice, our facial expressions, and our body language. When issuing a command or instructions to your child, or when you are correcting or disciplining them, the voice you use and your facial expression is extremely important. They need to be a different voice or expression than the one you use when you are just talking with them, praising them, or loving on them. I'm not saying you should be raising your voice. Actually, it is just the opposite. If you use a firm voice and a facial expression that is serious, you won't have to yell.

Let's say it is time for your toddler to get his or her bath. How do you tell them? Do you say, "Suzy, it's time for your bath, okay?" with a sweet, high-pitched voice and a big smile on your face? First of all, you should never use the word *okay* at the end of any of your requests or commands to your child. That tells them they are a part of the decision and have the option to decline. You are after all asking for their permission when you add the word *okay* to the end of your sentence. Parents do this without even realizing it. I often hear parents say things like, "We're going to go inside and have lunch now, okay?" to which the child will respond, "But I don't want to have lunch now!" When you use the word *okay*, you are encouraging a dialogue between yourself and your child. It is no longer a command. So when parents end up in exactly that, a dialogue with their child, they start getting impatient with them. But it is actually the parent's fault.

One side note regarding dialogue with your child. If you correct your child and they ask you why, it is okay to give them a reason for your decision once. We are after all trying to teach our children how to make decisions or why we make the decisions we make. But only give the answer to their question once. Some children might use your response to continue the dialogue by repeating "But why?" over and over again. Only give the answer to the *why* question once. If after that they keep asking you why, tell them "I already gave you an answer, I will not repeat myself again."

Instead, when you issue any command to your child, from the minor requests like "Please hand me your cup" or "Come here" to the more involved requests like "It's time for your bath or bedtime," your tone of voice should be lowered (not high-pitched), and firm and your facial expression should show that you are serious (not angry) and you mean it and disobedience is not an option. It should not be the same voice you use when you're loving on them or when you're, let's say, saying goodnight. There should be a difference, and they should be able to detect it. It might even help to practice in a mirror so you can see your facial expression and hear your voice.

After giving them a five-minute warning, come into the room calmly but firmly without smiling, but not frowning or angry, and state, "It's time for your bath now. Gather up your toys and let's go."

This would be the same voice you use to issue a command to your teenager. When asking them to take out the garbage or to come in for dinner or any other request you make of them, you should be firm with your voice, and your facial expressions need to show that you mean it.

I remember a time when a friend came to my home to give me help with decorating my master bedroom. She had to bring her two rambunctious toddler-age boys with her since her husband wasn't home to babysit. She was often frustrated because she had difficulty getting her children to listen to or obey her. As we were upstairs in the master bedroom bathroom, the boys suddenly appeared, immediately hopped up on my bed, and proceeded to repeatedly jump up and down on it. Now, I didn't let my own children jump on our furniture, let alone our bed, and I assumed my friend was going to correct them. I waited a minute or so, but to my dismay, she said nothing to them. So I leaned into the room and firmly but calmly said with a serious face, "Uh, boys, off the bed," and immediately they got down. Astonished, but almost relieved, my friend commented, "Boy, they really listen to you!" I didn't yell, and I wasn't angry, but they got the message loud and clear. There was no room for discussion—they were getting off my bed.

The same is true when just correcting your teenager's disrespectful attitude. You don't need to yell. Remain in control of the situation. Though it didn't happen often, I remember a time Elizabeth was getting an attitude of disrespect while talking with me. I firmly stated to her, "Lose the attitude, Elizabeth, you forget who you're talking to." She immediately changed her tone.

I often get feedback from amazed parents who took my parenting classes. When they put this simple rule into practice, they are astonished at the results they get as if it couldn't be that easy. One of the young moms who took my class couldn't wait to tell me the results she had when she started putting this rule into practice. She had told me while sitting in the class, her children often listened to her husband, but she was having difficulty getting them to listen to her when she issued a command. One day, her son was in the back seat of her car playing with his sippy cup, spilling it all over the seats. She asked him to hand it to her in her normal, pleasant voice. He just smiled and kept spilling the juice everywhere. Then she remembered what we discussed in the class and decided to give it a try. She looked at him with a serious expression and said firmly, "Steven [not his real name], hand me the cup!" Surprised but without hesitation, he handed her the cup. She couldn't believe it! "It worked!" she exclaimed happily.

So many times our children don't listen because we are unaware we are showing them by our tone of voice and facial expressions that they have the option to refuse us. We are not acting like the authority we are in their lives. They are often confused by us because the voice and expression we use when loving on them is the same voice we use when requesting something of them or correcting them. We come across as not really meaning what we say. We inadvertently give the impression they have an option to refuse us if they so choose.

Does this rule seem too simple to you? Are you asking if it could actually be that easy? I encourage you to try it and see for yourself.

Now, in the beginning of the book, I said these previous three rules—(1) "Never reward bad behavior," (2) "Always follow through," and (3) "How you say something is as important as what you say"— would help you to teach your kids to respect or "fear" you. As you reflect on it, hopefully you can see the parallels between applying the rules in your parenting and your child respecting you as the authority in their lives. If you never reward their bad behavior but instead make it cost them to disobey you, if you always follow through with those consequences consistently when they do disobey you and then always use a firm voice and facial expression when issuing a command or instructions, your child will learn from an early age to respect and obey you, always balancing it with lots of love and words of affirmation.

The last rule is the only rule that is not geared toward discipline per se but is equally important as the others. It is the rule that helps you balance out the discipline with love. While it's an equally important motivator for your child's obedience, it also helps you to build a healthy and affirming relationship with your child. I call it "Catch them being good."

Chapter 5

Rule #5: Catch Them Being Good

Positive reinforcement and praise is as equal a motivator to good behavior as discipline is but one that is often neglected by parents. Why? Because it's human nature to only notice when our children are acting up or disobeying. When they are behaving themselves or exhibiting good behavior, we don't notice or comment on it. Think about it. When was the last time your kids *weren't* fighting and you said, "Hey, it's great you guys aren't fighting and are getting along so well"? No, it's when they're in the other room ready to kill each other that we get involved.

But children need us to notice them and tell them we're proud of them when they do the right thing. Praise is a powerful motivator, not just for kids but adults as well. It makes us just as happy when our boss notices the good job we're doing at work and tells us so, doesn't it? Don't you just want to continue to do a good job when your boss notices the work you're doing? Children are the same way. Most children want to please their parents and want their parents to be proud of them. Praise is a huge encourager for them.

You might find that it takes a little practice to remember to do this rule. It usually is not something that comes naturally to us, but ask God for help in reminding you, and He will.

It is especially important to praise them when they are doing something you have been trying to teach them. In the early years of training up a child when your child is interacting with other children, try to be aware of how they are interacting, not only to see if anything needs improvement or correction but also to see positive things to encourage in them. If you have been trying to teach your toddler to share and you notice when they have a playdate that they are sharing their favorite toy with them, once the friend leaves, it is great if you let them know how proud you are that they shared and give them a big hug.

If you've been disciplining your teenagers because they haven't been treating their sibling very nicely and then you notice they are being kind to each other, sharing or encouraging each other, that is definitely something worth mentioning to them.

Obviously, we don't want to go overboard and praise them for every little thing they do. We don't want them to let this go to their head, nor do you want to make them think that every time they do the right thing, it will be noticed or praised. We need to teach them that sometimes they do the right thing without anyone but God noticing, because it's the right thing to do and He will reward them. But children need encouragement and praise to let them know you're proud of them. We all need that.

It's also good to occasionally praise them in front of other people when appropriate. Let's say your teenager scored the winning touchdown at the football game on Friday night, got a high score on the SATs, or won an award at school. Once in a while, mention it to a friend or grandparent while your teenager is present. You could say something like, "Susan won an award for spelling last week! We are so proud of her hard work!" This goes a long way to making them feel good about themselves and for them to know you're proud of them and their accomplishments.

Teenagers especially need to be encouraged in the difficult situations they might encounter through junior and senior high school. If you find out they didn't cheat on a test that others cheated on or didn't go to a party because they heard alcohol was going to be served, or came to the defense of someone who was being picked on or bullied in school, etc., you need to sit and talk with your teenager and tell them how proud you are of their choices and how much you understand how difficult that must have been for them. You also can and should pray with them for strength, encouragement, and help as they follow God and want to do the right thing.

I remember when my son, Daniel, was in junior high, some of his friends were going to see a movie that Daniel had read online had questionable sex scenes in it. He decided not to go. When he told me why he wasn't going, I hugged him and told him how proud I was of his decision and how hard it must have been to sit home on a Saturday night when his friends were all at the movies. I also told him God was proud of him too. We spent time with him that night hanging out together, which I think he appreciated.

Praise and encouragement are powerful motivators to good behavior, equally important as discipline and consequences.

CHAPTER 6

The Essentials

Once the Golden Rules are established in my parenting class, I go on to explain The *Three Essentials*. Though the main emphasis of this book is the five Golden Rules, and I discuss the essentials in greater detail in the class, I wanted to briefly touch on them in this chapter. They are almost as important as the Golden Rules, and an understanding of them goes hand in hand when they're used together.

The Three Essentials are as follows:

1. For discipline to be effective it must cost them.
2. Teach and be intentional.
3. Focus on shaping the heart and not just disciplining the behavior.

The first essential we already discussed in greater detail in chapter 3. That is, for discipline to be effective, it must cost them to misbehave. You need to be willing to use what matters most to them when you discipline.

The second essential in parenting is that *you must teach, and you must be intentional.* God never intended parenting to be a passive thing. Great kids don't just happen; they are instructed, disciplined, corrected, guided, challenged, and taught. The Bible says to "train up a child in the way they should go" (Proverbs 22:6). We need to teach them the way they should go.

If you want your child to be responsible, have a work ethic, be generous and unselfish, caring, appreciative, kind, love God and others, or any other qualities that come to mind, then you will have to be intentional and deliberate in teaching these things. They do not come naturally to children nor do they come with maturity.

It may sound exhausting, but you will have to be aware of the random teaching moments you are given each day and take advantage of them when they arise. You'll have to lean heavily on God and His Word and pray for lots of wisdom on how to teach them and what to say or do in specific situations. I go into greater detail of how to do this in the class.

The third essential in parenting is that much of *parenting should be focused on shaping the heart and not just disciplining the behavior.* Much of what I teach in the class shows you how to do this, but I'll touch on a few things here.

The Bible says if you change the heart you control the actions (Proverbs 4:23). This can be hard because we are usually so preoccupied with the external responses of our children. When a child is young (a toddler), parenting should be focused on simple obedience from the child. But as a child grows and enters the elementary school years, the focus needs to begin to gradually shift. During this time, a wise parent will not be looking just for outward obedience anymore but will also begin working toward a shaping of the heart, an internal heart change where your child is in agreement with God, His Word, and you about their behavior. Your relationship with your child at this age should also become more relational. Whereas when they are toddlers you expect obedience, as they age and begin to enter adolescence, you need to shift to more emphasis on relationship by explaining to them the decisions you're making and why. This teaches them how to make godly decisions themselves. Having more discussions with them about life situations they encounter and what a godly response might look like, according to God and His Word and why God says what He says in the Bible, is something that needs to occur regularly. They need to see you apply God's Word to their situation as you show them God's perspective on issues they are facing. Praying for them and with them is extremely important as they see you lean on Him for wisdom. They also need to see you living with biblical conviction in your own life. Kids can sense hypocrisy.

An example of this would be going to church and developing a relationship with Christ. When your child is young, you take them to church whether they want to go or not (obedience). But as the child grows older, you want them to go to church because they want to go and grow in their relationship with God. They want to know Him better, and their relationship with God becomes their own. It is a process that takes time, which is why God gives us at least eighteen years to do the job He has given us.

To do this, you have to get to the heart motivation behind their behavior, which many times will take wisdom from God. An example from my own childhood might help. When I was younger, my brother and I used to fight all the time. As punishment, our mother would make us write one hundred times, "I will not fight with my brother/sister." What she didn't know is when we got upstairs, my brother and I would turn it into a contest of who could finish each sentence first. It actually was fun. When we were done, she would proudly rip it up in front of us, thinking she made her point and we were going to stop fighting. I know she was doing the best she knew to do at the time, but she was more focused on our outward behavior (getting us to stop fighting) than our heart attitude toward each other. Because of this, her discipline did nothing to change our hearts or attitude, and without the heart change, there was no change in behavior. We continued to fight.

Knowing this, as I was raising my own children, I wanted my kids to be close and have a good relationship. So in addition to just praying for their relationship, I sought the Lord in how I might help bring this about. The end of the school year was always more difficult because my kids weren't used to being around each other all day. I remember two particularly difficult summers when they seemed to be fighting more than usual. So frustrated, I sent each one to their own rooms and sought God's guidance. Those two summers when I prayed, He impressed on my heart two different things each time. The first summer, it was to make them write "Why I love my brother/sister and why I'm glad God gave her/him to me." I told them it had to be at least one full page, and they each had to read what they wrote to the other when they were done. My daughter barely made it through reading the letter she wrote to her brother before she burst into tears. Before you knew it, they were hugging and apologizing to each other. It seemed to help mend things for the rest of that summer.

The following summer, when I sought God about their fighting, I sensed Him telling me to make them pray together every night. Only there were to be ground rules. They could only pray for the other person, not themselves, and each one had to tell the other what they needed prayer for. It's hard to be angry with someone when you have to humble yourself and tell them your prayer needs, and it's also hard to be angry with someone when you are lifting them and their needs to God in prayer. They did this every night for at least a month or two, and not only did they stop fighting, but I could see them getting closer and more caring and understanding toward each other by the time summer drew to a close and beyond.

Another reason the heart doesn't change is that often parents don't think through the consequences they give their children and, as I mentioned before, have a "one size fits all" mentality about discipline. They might send their child to their room for every offense, ground them every time they disobey, or resort to spanking for every infraction. Why do we do this? Because it can be tiresome to think through the consequences and how to make the punishment fit the crime. An example of this would be what I mentioned earlier in chapter 3, if you have a teenager who won't work or hold down a job. A consequence that fits might be they can't go to the movies with friends or get the shoes or clothes they want because they don't have the money they need to buy them. In this example, the consequence coincides with and relates to the behavior.

One side note, your teenager's obedience to "Because I said so" is not success, and you should rarely, if ever, be using those words as you raise your junior or senior high school-age child. As I said previously, you need to become more relational with your teenager, discussing why one choice is better than another biblically or why you are making a decision you are making. I once had a father confide, while dropping his daughter off at my home for senior high small groups, that she had made plans to go to a party that night. His daughter had told him she didn't want to go to small groups. He told her, "Cancel your plans; you're going to small groups." He felt he had succeeded because she came to our senior high activity, but I can tell you with pretty much certainty that although her body was there, her heart was not. This is not success.

A better way would be to have a conversation with his daughter about what she was feeling and why. He also could've encouraged her with why it is important to go to youth group functions; God says in His Word, believers need to fellowship together to build each other up and encourage one another to edify her and help her grow in her walk with God. Also, God might use her in someone else's life if she makes herself available by going. It also would've been a great time to pray with her. If she still seems dead set against going, I wouldn't force her to. I would instead consider taking her out to do something fun together to grow your relationship or stay home as a family to do a fun activity together. Privately, I would pray for her. I'd ask God to help her to do a work in her heart and change her heart about going to youth group in the future so that she would want to go.

As our children get older, we want the heart to change from just obeying us to instead wanting to do the right thing and make godly choices on their own.

We discuss in greater detail how to accomplish this in the class. But if you're unable to attend a class and have any questions about anything you have read, included at the back of this book is my e-mail contact information. I'd be more than happy to chat with you and discuss any questions you may have about the things you have read or regarding your own parenting issues.

EPILOGUE

Encouragement for Parents

I reflect back on our years raising our children. In some ways, it seems like yesterday, and in other ways, it seems a lifetime ago. For me, the hardest years were the infant/toddler years, though each stage had its challenges. As I think about the toddler years as a stay-at-home mom, I remember the isolation and loneliness I felt. My life at times seemed to be the worst combination of repetitiveness and monotony. Not only did my duties not challenge me mentally, but they had to be done repeatedly, over and over again. I would change a diaper only to have to change another a short time later. It seems I would just get the breakfast dishes put away when I was pulling them out for lunch and then again for dinner. I felt like nothing was ever completed. There was no way to gauge my progress. My life seemed to be defined by the prefix *re-*. Rewipe little fingers and mouths after meals, remop the same floor, rewash the same dishes or clothes, redust the same furniture, recook the same meals, etc. etc.

The junior high and senior high school years presented a whole new set of challenges. Not only were things hectic as we tried to balance crazy schedules of sports, ballet, school activities, and homework, but it was challenging to be more relational and present in the moment with our kids to be aware of daily opportunities God gave us to teach concepts from His Word and apply them to common everyday experiences in their lives. That took much prayer and wisdom from God.

Especially frustrating at times was trying to gauge our progress in parenting. A concept we were trying to teach would go unnoticed, or worse yet, they would seem to take hold of it one day only to let go of it the next. Three steps forward, two steps back, to our dismay. Many times I felt in the big scheme of things what we did didn't matter and/or wasn't making a difference (maybe it was, but I couldn't tell). At times, I'd find myself reflecting to days long ago when I worked outside the home. Even if my boss didn't praise me often, at least once a year I would be called into his office for a review of my work and receive words of approval and a raise. It seemed more black and white, cut and dry back then.

One of the challenges with raising children is you often don't get to see the full results of your hard work for eighteen years. Yes, God is gracious. He gives you glimpses of His grace in the growth and maturing of your children over time. But your job isn't finished yet, so you go on—two steps forward, three steps back. It's really only when they finally leave for college or get a job on their own one day that you get to see the full reward for all your hard work and if what you tried to teach them and instill in them stuck.

The Bible says, "If we are faithful with little we will be given much" (Matthew 25:23). No, I'm not saying it is a little thing to raise children, but the job we have will seem at times insignificant or unproductive in the big scheme of life. God loves you and cares about who you are and all that you are trying to do in raising your children in the obscurity of your home when no one but Him is looking. He asks for your faithfulness in these years. It matters to God if you're doing your best to honor Him in the way you run your household, stay on a budget, take care of your home, provide for your family, and raise, discipline, and train up your children "in the way they should go" (Proverbs 22:6). He sees, cares, and greatly desires to help you if you will only ask Him. He knows you can't do this job without His guidance, strength, and wisdom. But you have to invite Him into your parenting. He promises to greatly rewarded you one day in more ways than one, if you remain faithful. Chuck Swindoll says, "You must cultivate the habit of doing little things well. That is when God puts iron into your bones. The test of my calling is how well I do when no one is looking. It is in the schoolroom of solitude and obscurity that we learn to become men and women of God."

Raising children to know, love, and follow God and to love others is the toughest job there is. It takes great determination on your part and dependency on God for strength and wisdom, and much prayer! You have been entrusted with the most important and valuable assignment on the planet: raising the next generation for God (and others). Don't let anyone tell you otherwise.

We are now on the flip side of raising our own children. My daughter is a wife and teacher now; she and my son-in-law reside in another town. My son, a college graduate, is on staff at our church—a young man of twenty-five. There aren't little faces to wipe anymore, toys to trip over, diapers to change, or spills to clean up. The house is quieter, stays cleaner longer, and those challenging years are a distant memory. But I smile a smile of satisfaction every time I spend time with my "kids." Were those years at times challenging? Yes. Were those years worth the hard work? A thousand times YES! I don't regret, and you won't ever regret investing in the lives of your children or the sacrifices you are making now. Not only that, you will have many times when you will wish them back. The years go by too quickly. When you see the responsible, caring, kind, generous, loving, and godly adults they have become and you realize you, with God's help, had a part in that, you will know it was all worth it. In the meantime, "press on toward the goal for the prize" (Philippians 3:14) and "fight the good fight" (2 Timothy 4:7). What you are doing matters, has eternal consequences, and you will reap the rewards if you faint not (Hebrews 12:3).

God bless you,

Michele

About the Author

Michele and her husband, Chris, have been married for more than thirty years and have two grown children together. They attend Calvary Chapel of Philadelphia. Chris and Michele were teaching parents for teenage boys at a Christian home for children. Michele also taught parenting classes at a local Christian maternity home. She presently enjoys being a mom mentor for MOPS International at a local church. Michele launched her Legacy Parenting Class in the fall of 2013. In addition to teaching the parenting classes, she has a passion for mentoring parents one-on-one. Michele and Chris live in Horsham, Pennsylvania.

Contact Information
E-mail address: legacyparentingclass@gmail.com
Website: www.legacyparentingclass.org

CPSIA information can be obtained
at www.ICGtesting.com
Printed in the USA
BVHW03s1325060918
526717BV00001B/21/P